This book is dedicated to all of my beautiful grandchildren. It was after seeing all of you and your greatness over the course of a few days that the desire to share greatness with everyone became reality.

Acknowledgments and gratitude

Thank you to my parents for creating me

Thank you to my four wonderful children and their families for sharing your life with me. Thank you to Maya for typing this.

Thank you to my friends Karen, Amy, Pam, Judy M, Carol and Carolyn for being there and listening and sharing your life with me.

Thank you to those who have passed through my life at the exact time I needed them.

Sally Kauffman

WISHING YOU GREATNESS

iUniverse books may be ordered through booksellers or by contacting:

iUniverse
1663 Liberty Drive
Bloomington, IN 47403
www.iuniverse.com
1-800-Authors (1-800-288-4677)

ISBN: 978-1-4917-9082-3 (sc)
ISBN: 978-1-4917-9083-0 (e)

Library of Congress Control Number: 2016906874

Print information available on the last page.

iUniverse rev. date: 5/10/2016

Introduction

The intention for this book was

For my grandson.

I am so very proud of him for his journey.

After he graduated high school, he tried a technical school. It was a challenge and he had a great learning curve to overcome. However, every time I texted him or called him, he always responded the same way, I'm great. When I would ask how everything was going, his response was great! I don't know if he sent it to me to make me feel better or if he really meant it. So Jeremy go out in the world with your greatness.

As I began writing I realized that everyone's journey should be with greatness every day. Here are many ways to remind ourselves, our families, our loves ones, our friends, our neighbors and the world about our greatness

How to use the Book

Read every page

Open it up to any page when you need a lift

Share it with someone

Live with your greatness everyday

Use this as inspiration to move you in the direction of your desires and dreams

Remind someone to live in their greatness

Add more of your own personal greatness at the back of the book

Enjoy your journey

"Be not afraid of greatness: some are born great, some achieve greatness and some have greatness thrust upon them"

(Quote Act II, Scene V)
William Shakespeare Twelfth Night

Chapter One

Being in Greatness

Be an ambassador for your greatness

Be an example of greatness

Be astounding with your greatness

Be authentic in your greatness

Be aware of your greatness

Be awesome with your greatness

Be awe-inspiring with your greatness

Be beautiful in your greatness

Be brilliant in your greatness

Be clear in your greatness

Be compassionate in your greatness

Be enchanted by your greatness

Be energetic with your greatness

Be extravagant with your greatness

Be fantastic with your greatness

Be fascinated by your greatness

Be first class with your greatness

Be gorgeous with your greatness

Be grateful for your greatness

Be grateful in greatness

Be healthy in your greatness

Be honest with your greatness

Be humble with your greatness

Be in abundance with your greatness

Be incredible with your greatness

Be independent with your greatness

Be insightful with your greatness

Be inspired by your greatness

Be kind to yourself with your greatness

Be legendary with your greatness

Be magical in your greatness

Be mindfulness of your greatness

Be on top of the world with your greatness

Be one with your greatness

Be out of the world with your greatness

Be outrageous with your greatness

Be patient with your greatness

Be peachy with your greatness

Be phenomenal with your greatness

Be positive with your greatness

Be present in your greatness

Be purposeful with your greatness

Be royal in your greatness

Be smart in your greatness

Be spectacular with your greatness

Be spontaneous with your greatness

Be the best you can be in your greatness

Be the first one to support the greatness of others

Be thrilled in your greatness

Be triumphant with your greatness

Be truthful with your greatness

Be vulnerable with your greatness

Be wild with your greatness

Be yourself in your greatness

Chapter 2

Doing Greatness

Befriend your greatness

Adore with greatness

Affirm your greatness

Allow yourself to fulfill your greatness

Anticipate your greatness

Appreciate your greatness

Ask for your greatness

Ask others to share their greatness

Awaken in your greatness

Cheer the world with your greatness

Choose your greatness wisely

Color your world with greatness

Comfort others in your greatness

Commit to your greatness

Communicate your greatness with zest and zeal

Connect with your greatness

Create a loving environment with your greatness

Dance with greatness

Douse yourself in greatness

Delight in your greatness

Demonstrate your greatness to others

Desire your greatness

Don't substitute anything for your greatness

Donate time to your greatness

Electrify the world with your greatness

Embody your greatness

Embrace your greatness

Enjoy greatness

Enjoy the greatness of life

Enjoy your challenges with your greatness

Exercise your greatness

Exercise yourself in your greatness

Expand your greatness

Explore your greatness

Fall in love with your greatness

Feel fabulous in your greatness

Feel the beauty in your greatness

Feel your greatness in the moment

Find pleasure in greatness

Find rupture in your greatness

Flourish in greatness

Flourish in your greatness

Fly in your greatness

Follow your path of greatness

Gift yourself your greatness

Give out blessings with your greatness

Give thanks for your greatness

Give with greatness

Give yourself space with your greatness

Glow in your greatness

Grow with your greatness

Handle each moment with your greatness

Harmonize in greatness

Have an attitude of greatness

Have hope with your greatness

Head up tall in your greatness

Heal yourself with greatness

Honor your greatness

Honor yourself with your greatness

Immerse yourself in greatness

Indulge in your greatness

Join with others with your greatness

Juice up your greatness

Jump for joy of your greatness

Jump in greatness

Laugh with greatness

Lavish in your greatness

Lead to greatness

Learn by your greatness

Listen to your greatness

Live in wonder with your greatness

Live your greatness

Lounge in greatness

Love and accept your greatness

Love your greatness

Love your greatness in harmony with nature

Make a legacy of your greatness

Make greatness your motto

Make greatness your passion

Make way for others greatness

Make wise choices in your greatness

Make your greatness contagious

Manifest your greatness

Marinate in your greatness

Meditate in greatness

Meditate with your greatness

Mirror your greatness

Own your greatness

Party with your greatness

Picnic with your greatness

Plant the earth with your greatness

Rap with your greatness

Receive with greatness

Receive your greatness

Reflect on your greatness

Rejoice in others greatness

Relax in your greatness

Relish in your greatness

Remember your greatness

Remember your roots of greatness

Rest in your greatness

Revitalize in your greatness

Rise up in your greatness

Rock and roll with your greatness

Seduce yourself in greatness

Set an example with your greatness

Share with greatness

Share your emotions and feelings with your greatness

Share your greatness in art

Share your greatness with humanity

Shine in your greatness

Shout out to the world your greatness

Shout your greatness

Show a willingness to learn in your greatness

Show gratitude for your greatness

Show tenderness in your greatness

Show the world your greatness

Show wisdom in your greatness

Show your greatness in your work

Sing with greatness

Slather yourself with your greatness

Sleep in greatness

Smile as your greatness surrounds you

Smile with your greatness

Soak up your greatness

Soothe your fears in greatness

Speak of your greatness

Spread your wings in your greatness

Stand up and salute your greatness

Step forward in your greatness

Study in greatness

Succeed in your greatness

Surprise yourself with your greatness

Surrender to your greatness

Take each day as it comes in your greatness

Tell the world of your greatness

Treat your body with greatness

Trust in your greatness

Uplift those around you in your greatness

Use your greatness to express yourself

Use your imagination with your greatness

Visualize your greatness

Work for peace with your greatness

Work in greatness

Write your greatness

Chapter 3

Let your Greatness...

Let your greatness be your inspiration

Let your greatness be your youth

Let your greatness always be the right time and place for you

Let your greatness be a blessing

Let your greatness be meaningful

Let your greatness be remembered

Let your life flow in grace with your greatness

Let your miracles be of greatness

Let your soul feel your greatness

Chapter 4
Greatness

Greatness is the beginning of your success

Greatness leads to a good laugh

Greatness leads to dreams

Greatness will keep you going

Greatness will live forever

Greatness will make you smile

There is joy in greatness

Growth is greatness

I love you for your greatness

Life gets better daily with greatness

Life is full of greatness

Life=greatness=love

Originality forms your greatness

Wherever you are, let your greatness shine

Wishing you Greatness

Chapter 5

Write your own greatness

About the author

Sally is a mother of four and a grandmother to ten and another on the way. She is a nurse for over forty years and a school nurse for twenty-nine of those years. Sally has spent the last few years in the evenings, weekends and summers discovering and continuing to learn about her passion. She lives near the city of Philadelphia.

Wishing you greatness

Do you need to be reminded of your greatness? Do you want to move toward your dreams and desires of greatness? How about reminding your loves ones, family friends and coworkers to live in their greatness every day?

Whether you know it or not, we all have a touch of greatness that we can experience in our lives every single day.

This is your inspiration for greatness. Read it all, pick it up every day or just pick a page

Enjoy your journey to greatness

Edwards Brothers Malloy
Thorofare, NJ USA
January 5, 2017